Table of Contents Y0-DBU-579

Welcome to your 50s, please pass the wine and a chiropractic and Botox referral. Thank you.

Introduction

Your 20s, 30s, and now 40s are over. Permanently, it seems. You have been a walking, talking, working human for decades now. You've eaten your vegetables (or not), nourished and been nourished by family and friends, and even have learned mindfulness.

Somehow, through no fault of your own, you have your 50th birthday (or another significant one) coming up – or you've already passed that milestone. The least you deserve is a good laugh – or better yet, lots of them. Think of this book as bedtime stories for your over-the-hill self.

Acknowledgements

Much gratitude for the love and support of my family – particularly my son and daughter-in-law who are closing in on 50 as this book goes to press. Watching them navigate this stage of life has been a fun research-in-the-wild experience.

And to my husband who had to listen to a zillion iterations of each chapter and never once said, for the love of god, just be quiet. His encouragement and patience – to say nothing of his enthusiasm for DoorDash (because let's face it, how much was I cooking during this period?) – contributed positively to the entire process.

Next, a special shout-out to the Barnes & Noble managers (you know who you are!) who accepted my first humor book as part of their then-brand-new local authors program. Seeing my book displayed for the first time in a bookstore that I have loved my entire life has been an absolute thrill.

Christine Mallouf, the wonderful artist who has illustrated both of my humor books, has been a total joy to work with. Somehow her incredible abilities as an artist are combined with the most warm, flexible, and generous spirit one can imagine.

Betty Watson, the designer who has done the graphics for both books, did an awesome job of making this text come to life. I am most appreciative of her creativity and talent.

And finally, dear reader, you are who this entire effort is about! I appreciate you tremendously and hope you not only find this book funny – I hope it makes you feel warm, almost as if you are being hugged by someone who "gets" you. Midlife can be a most wonderful time and to make it so, you need to design it according to your wants and needs. *Your* wants and needs. Make sure you know what they are and then go after them. Take good care of your heart and your head – if you do, most of the rest will follow.

We're sorry to inform you that . . .

YOUR FORTIES ARE OVER

WRITTEN BY **Renee Burns Lonner**

ILLUSTRATED BY **Christine Mallouf**

CHAPTER 1

OMG
That Can't Be
MY
Neck – Make It Stop!

Nora Ephron* nailed it, for sure.

Except for one teeny, tiny, very small thing – your neck becomes the focus of your attention only after you recover from the fact that your mother now inhabits your mirror and is staring back at you.

Actually she has been doing this for a few years. *And she doesn't even live in your house.* Clearly, she can be in two places at once, as she has always claimed.

Your neck in the mirror is bad enough, but then there is your neck on Zoom (thank you, pandemic).

That neck is a wattle-in-the-making.

Couldn't they have thought of a less obnoxious word than wattle? Would that have killed anyone? Wattle sounds like the ugliest-ever offspring of waddle and cattle.

OK, back to this whole face-neck thing. It's no wonder we need so many creams. Face cream, eye cream and, for heaven's sake, neck cream. To say nothing of creams for other places.

Which brings up a brand-new concern: *What happens if I put one of my zillion creams in the wrong place?* Just ponder that for a minute. So scary I can't even imagine.

Enough about your face, moving on. Remember your high school bio class? Sure you do, that class was fascinating.

Let's do a system-by-system refresher course so we can talk about your *insides* in an organized fashion. Here is a reminder of the systems of the body: circulatory, respiratory, skeletal, digestive, and nervous. How about we start with the one with the best name, the nervous system?

I'm kidding, of course! This is a humor book, what were you thinking?

Biggest take-aways – First, gravity is *not* your friend. (That's putting it mildly – in fact, gravity is now enemy number ONE!)

Second, **for the frequent insult of having to see your pretend-listening face on Zoom**, consider exploring Zoom's "studio effects" magic. Don't go crazy and make yourself look like you've had major "work" done and you couldn't smile even if you wanted to. Just adjust a little here and there. Couldn't hurt.

Studio effects will do nothing, however, for your eyes or teeth. For these two body parts, Darwin is flashing the yellow caution light. Darwin sucks.

If you had and still have perfect distance and reading vision, we hate you and you're weird. The rest of us need LASIK or a collection of different glasses for reading and various other tasks.

Please note that you look like a dumbass squinting every time you try to read a label in a store, so just go to CVS and get reading glasses for every room in your house – and another pair for your bag. Comes in handy if you want to read a menu in a restaurant, especially those menus with light grey print on a white background.

Oh, and it only gets worse. But don't worry – when you get even older, cataract surgery will save your ass (and your eyes).

As for **teeth**, those of you with perfect teeth that are showing no signs of age need to move on (probably to another book). While evolution has not caught up with the fact that we are living longer and want to look decent when we smile, dentists and endodontists sure have!

Welcome to the decade of crowns, too bad they are not the lovely ones that go on your head. No, these usually follow a root canal. **Fillings are so 20th century.**

Lastly, for those few of you who are looking for *actual advice* about your general health given your advanced years, you are welcome to read our humble suggestions below.

For the rest of you, just turn to Chapter 2.

Short

(boring, we know) list:

▶ **Prioritize sleep.**
Yes, I mean daily (nightly). "Catching up" on sleep is not a thing.

Riddle:
What do you call a physician who does not listen to you and is an arrogant jerk?

Answer:
Your *former doctor*.

▶ **Diets don't work.** You know this. Stop it and focus on your health.

▶ **Drink less alcohol.** (I said this list was annoying, you were warned.) Your brain can handle less than it did in your forever-lost youth.

▶ **De-toxify your relationships.** We can handle less stress as we age, and here's one good and most effective way to decrease it: keep close those people who love and respect you, and keep a good distance from the rest.

✱ For those of you who saw your mother reading Nora's book but don't know it firsthand, in 2008 Nora Ephron wrote a classic on women, necks and midlife, "I Feel Bad About My Neck: And Other Thoughts On Being A Woman."

Medical Escapades, or
WHY
Is It So Damn Hot in Here?!

Just look at you, nice and shiny and solidly middle aged –

You're ready for your first
Co·lon·os·co·py!

That is, unless you have other issues and have already had one. We'll start with the newbies: **Put on your big girl panties (oops, I mean take them off)**, this procedure is really not a biggie.

Or rather, it's only a biggie in your mind where it engenders abject terror. So misplaced.

Spend that energy on the climate disaster, world hunger, or ongoing wars in the Middle East. This particular midlife issue isn't worth the drama.

WHY?

Because the prep involves drinking a liquid that tastes like a cross between Kool Aid and Tilex (that's the worst part), a few trips to the bathroom (like an intestinal bug without being

sick) and some hunger, but **then you get the best drugs in the world** as they send you off to dreamland.

When you wake up, you can have all the **food you've hallucinated about** during the previous 24 hours. Then you can go back to sleep in your own bed and feel totally justified in **not doing one damn thing for the next 24 hours.**

After all, you need to "sleep it off." Even if you feel just fine, which you probably will.

This advice to "calm down and just do it" is coming to you from the Colonoscopy Queen. That's right, I've had nearly a dozen of them. Seems my colon, which should be busy enough doing its regular job, has a side hustle growing polyps (yuk).

Tips from the Colonoscopy Queen

- Calm down and just do it.
- Procedure is painless.
- Regular colonoscopies are key to prevention/early detection of cancer.

My doc told me early on that regular colonoscopies were about the only way to actually prevent cancer in that lovely area and that was enough motivation for me.

So don't be an ass (though this is all about your ass and nothing else), one of those people who spend a decade or two whining to their friends about how terrified or phobic they are about the process. Because when you do it, you are going to be SO embarrassed about what a non-event it was.

And if something bad happens in the meantime, before you do it, you are going to feel guilty and dumb, and your family and friends are not just going to be upset. They are going to have to try to suppress their urge to tell you **this could have been prevented**.

Moving on to the other medical fun stuff that comes with being 50 and beyond — menopause, hot flashes, and brain fog. Geez, bet you can hardly wait! Not much humor here, but lots of female bonding opportunities with friends.

Think your arms no longer look great in sleeveless shirts?

Think again. Who the hell cares what you look like if your body suddenly feels like it's in a pizza oven? It's sleeveless shirts or no shirt (better yet, no bra). And a shirt – even one that shows your less-than-totally-firm arms – sounds like a more civilized option.

And please tell me why that **sudden feeling** that causes sweat to drip down your back, makes you turn red in the face (bye-bye make-up), and lasts an interminable amount of time, is called a hot "flash?" **A "flash"** should be here and gone in an instant, no? WTF?

Oh wait, I think I understand. It causes you to want to flash, to take off all your clothes, as in indecent exposure! That's it! Because when it comes on, it hardly matters where you are – restaurant, dinner party, wherever. The waiter asks for your order and your answer is **"For god's sake, could you guys turn on the AC?!"**

I could write another whole book about my suspicion that if menopause happened to men, there would have been awesome drugs a long time ago. Think the opposite of Viagra – this is about turning down the heat!

Yes, you will have more doctor appointments in midlife than you have had since you were a child. You will become so familiar with your skin doc that you will give them the affectionate term "my derm."

Your derm will spend most of their time trying to sell you on cosmetic procedures because, like you, they do not want to deal with insurance companies.

Remember those years — no decades — of thinking that the sun was healthy and a good tan was evidence thereof?

Yeah, well, whoever said that was wrong.

 You can try communicating this news bulletin to your kids or nieces and nephews as they head to the beach. They will probably listen about as well as you did at that age. Which means they have their fingers in their ears. Or a particular middle finger where you can't see it.

Advice you have not asked for and probably do not want: **Conscientious (not obsessive) medical care** is an essential part of self-care. **Boo.** And boring.

Just do it and don't make it your identity. There is no good reason to use that wonderful lunch with a girlfriend you haven't seen in a year for a complete rundown of the body parts that do not function precisely as well as they did 20 years ago and which specialists you need to see to tune those suckers up.

Focus on happier topics — like how technology is ruining kids' minds, the collapse of the educational system, or the possibility of another pandemic. So much more appetizing.

CHAPTER 3

Never Mind Your Body,
YOUR MIND
Is an Awesome Thing!

So while you are spending much of your time trying to find underwear that fits your . . . umm, differently arranged middle parts, **your head has become much more settled.** Maybe even mature (but let's not get carried away).

Learning from experience can be a difficult and unpleasant thing, but **second-hand learning is totally awesome**. That's when you learn from the amazingly stupid things your friends do or even consider doing. Like treks down and up the Grand Canyon (on their feet), going to a dude ranch for two weeks to herd cattle, or eating street food in a country that has not heard of food safety.

Here, **magically** you change your **Zoom pretend-listening face** to a pretend-sympathetic face while your friend describes the absolutely predictable outcome of one of these adventures.

You work at not sounding judgmental, smug, or god forbid, amused. **After all, you are now in your fifties.** All you have to say in response to an invitation to partake in an adventure guaranteed to land you at urgent care at best or, at worst, the ER, is **"Are you f**king kidding me?" Done.**

Gone are the days when you listened to Jessica telling you how she was nearly **air-lifted out of a third world country** after breaking her leg dismounting from an elephant without much of a ladder – because she was the only one in her group who had to pee half-way through the morning adventure – and you think "Well, that's typical Jessica – careless and uncoordinated. I am neither of those things."

No, the balloon over your now mature, non-omnipotent and

GEEZ... ANOTHER DUMBASS BREAKS A LEG!

scared-when-you-should-be head reads "Jessica, you need to stop doing things that you should have done in your 20s. For heaven's sake, Jessica, you're 50!"

We're not suggesting you take your next vacation with Road Scholar. No, you're decades away (well, maybe one decade) from even considering that. Instead, ponder a sane, guided African Safari adventure, where the only thing that stands between a charging tiger and your being the entrée at dinner is the guy at the back of the Jeep with a rifle. Hope he's a good shot.

And speaking of judgment, the **need to check-in** with others before making an everyday decision has evaporated – **Poof!**

The following
???????
no longer occur to you:

▶ Does this dress make my already big boobs look bigger**?**

▶ I wanna wear white in April to that major event, do you think it's okay**?**

▶ Does this color make me look jaundiced**?**

Because by now **you really don't care what others think.** Including your partner, spouse, or best friend. Don't like this shirt? Think my new handbag is beyond hideous, that whoever designed it had to be on crack, and that even looking at it gives you motion sickness?

Sorry you feel that way — because I love it!

Now to be clear, we're not suggesting that you avoid expert opinions on important subjects. That would be dumb.

No, we're talking about making everyday decisions yourself, decisions that younger women regard as a Gallup poll opportunity.

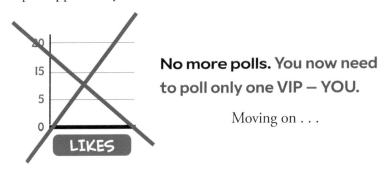

No more polls. You now need to poll only one VIP — YOU.

Moving on . . .

Another source of learning you may have sought out is therapy, as well as therapeutic tools like yoga, mindfulness, and meditation.

Unlike when you were significantly younger, you now recognize that it takes strength to ask for help and wisdom to use it. **Give yourself permission to use all the f**king help you can get.** Navigating this midlife adult thing with some measure of sanity (forget grace) is not easy.

CHAPTER 4

Toasting
(OR ROASTING)
Family and Friends

Family – you know, those people you can't wait to spend, say, 15 or 20 minutes with – now includes three generations for many. And **WOW, what a difference a generation makes!**

Your parents' parenting style simply may have been described as more on the **permissive or strict** side – or quickly moving from one to the other depending on whether the transgression was your coming home an hour late or their discovering the pot you had been hiding for months in plain sight in your room.

You, on the other hand, have had **so many choices** in terms of raising these kiddos and you have discussed each and every parenting decision with your girlfriends. Also, often, with your partner.

You certainly do not want to be a lawnmower, bulldozer, **helicopter** or, at the other extreme end, free-range **parent** (no, this is not a reference to cage-free chickens and our huge concern about their quality of life and mental state before we kill and eat them.) Or a jellyfish, dolphin, or tiger parent.

Seems that our culture has decided that you can choose, as a parent, to be insulted by a comparison to heavy equipment or to animals of varying intelligence levels.

Then there are the bat-shit crazy parenting styles of your friends – watching some of these styles in action tests your sanity, to say nothing of your basic social skills. Relax, your parenting drives them nuts, too.

Here's an idea: you can all go to therapy together and watch the therapist try to walk the line between providing realistic feedback and avoiding the parents' or kids' wrath. This is essentially a high-wire act without a net. Or Simone Biles' performance on the balance beam, except much less awesome.

Then there is the subject of divorce and co-parenting and how you may be navigating this old or more recent biggie as your **kids get ready to fly the coop**.

Some advice to offer as you are breathing a sigh of relief and contemplating the wonderful world in which you will no longer have to communicate regularly with your former partner: Stop relaxing and prepare for when your college freshman, or child with their first real job, calls and asks what to do about their closest friend's current (and very real) crisis.

Spoiler alert: No, the correct answer is *not* "Call your mother/father/older sibling/dorm advisor/haven't had coffee yet."

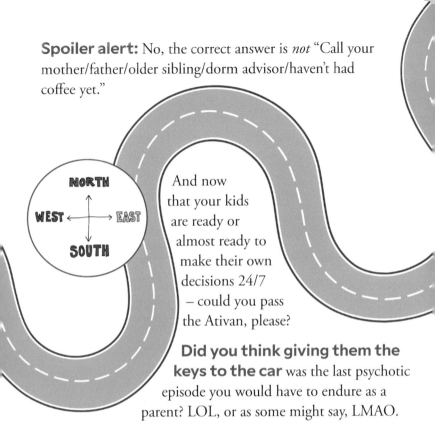

And now that your kids are ready or almost ready to make their own decisions 24/7 – could you pass the Ativan, please?

Did you think giving them the keys to the car was the last psychotic episode you would have to endure as a parent? LOL, or as some might say, LMAO.

For those headed to college or to a program or job in another city or state, their driving is nothing compared to placing *every single* life decision in their hands.

Parenting is forever. Full stop. Married, single, divorced, whatever, the kids need you as parents forever. So buck up and appreciate that you are surviving or have survived their adolescence and take time to indulge your long-term revenge fantasies about when they are parents of teens. Does that make you wanna do everything you can to be alive and coherent by that time? Hell yes!! **OMG, I'm salivating already!**

Now for a silly segue. These are the same children, let us remember, who did not need to learn – literally – how to tie their shoes. Or write in cursive. Let's take shoes first. Remember your parents telling you to tie your shoes before you left the house? Ha! So 20th century.

This is the Velcro generation and **IMHO**, colleges could learn a lot more about problem-solving ability in their candidates if they dropped the SATs and just asked them to demonstrate shoe-tying. That's a whole skill set. Yes, he no longer needs to make the bunny ears as the first step and also, yes, he aced honors math and science in high school – your point?

Back to shoes. Here, it turns out that manufacturers smelled the envy of parents and began offering zillions of choices of **"slip-ons" for adults**. How lazy are we becoming? The answer – very. Within a generation, the slogan of one popular shoe brand may be "Just don't do it."

Or maybe universities should scrap the SATs and, instead, **ASK the kids** to make out a shopping list in cursive. What's that, they ask –

"Cursive? Just hand me my phone so I can **ASK Siri WTF cursive is!**"

Returning to friends, many are living their best lives as single women. Your generation – and hopefully, all future ones – has had the smarts to **honor their choice** and more importantly, them.

To be fair, some of you who are partnered have drooled as they text photos from their hiking, cruise, or yoga weekends. Others of you might think, you don't know what you're missing!

For example, your daughter's new boyfriend could be a hot mess and she could be totally allergic to your advice about him (or anything else). And you're thinking, could I slip birth control pills in her food? To add to that, your ex-husband may have decided that his first midlife crisis was so fun he's doing it again!

Your life is just plain awesome!

Just be glad you did not settle for mediocre, as your parents' generation often did. Mediocre as a thing needs to be reserved for Trader Joe's latest chicken pot pie, the **new Italian restaurant down the street**, or the veggie burger you made last night. Not for major relationships – that would be insane. And you are not insane, just hot all the time!

Before we leave the subject of your own transition to midlife and all its pleasures and move on to the larger culture (ew), we thought you might enjoy setting the **Circle of Life** wheel (it's not a real wheel, but you get the idea) on the next page to your personal reality, this minute. Feel free to reset it in five minutes.

Circle of Life

Readers, transition lenses, contacts, WTF?!

My straight hair got curly overnight – help!

When do teenage girls become human again?

Can I tell Kate her new boyfriend sucks?

My favorite restaurant is too noisy.

I'm exhausted, the kids go to bed way past my bed time.

Too old for high heels, too young for a podiatrist.

I'm doing keto and pilates – oh metabolism, where art thou?

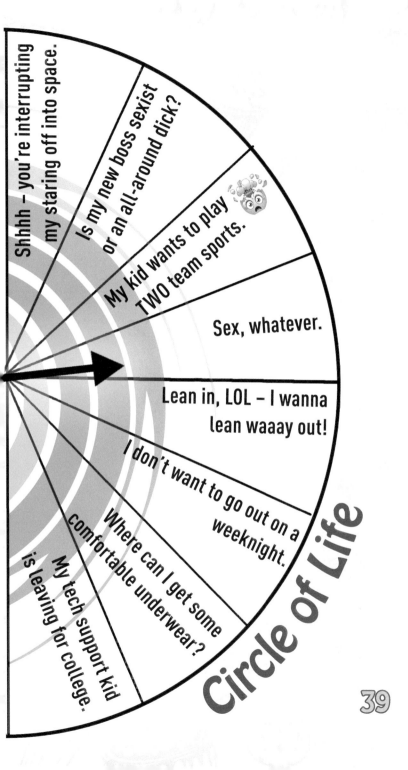

Shhhh – you're interrupting my staring off into space.

Is my new boss sexist or an all-around dick?

My kid wants to play TWO team sports.

Sex, whatever.

Lean in, LOL – I wanna lean waaay out!

I don't want to go out on a weeknight.

Where can I get some comfortable underwear?

My tech support kid is leaving for college.

Circle of Life

CHAPTER 5

Your Culture, As You
KNEW IT —
Going, Going, Gone!

As should be clear by now, **you are special** and have a **unique place between the older generation** who saw the advent of television and the younger folks we affectionately refer to as digital natives. That is a huge span and **you are the bridge**. You have an awesome responsibility – use it well.

With that, we are almost at the end of this book. Before we close, let's take a quick look at our **culture through drawings** – sort of a mini-culturama (perhaps a made-up word, not sure). Enjoy . . . and be sure to read the Afterword.

Welcome to fifty and beyond!

You are invited . . .

. . . To come as you are

(because really, when
was the last time you
wore real clothes?)

Bye-Bye hip cool and young

Welcome
to Fifty

45

Afterword

Or afterthoughts.

Or just freakin' read this page before you close the book.

Billy Joel, **a musical legend** who is now 74 years old, happens to be on tour throughout the country as this book goes to press. The moving lyrics he wrote in **"Vienna"** provide a metaphor for aging, as well as a poignant warning. **He nailed it all** in this song.

My personal translation of those lyrics – since my attorney tells me that no way, no how, can I quote them in this book – goes something like this: You're halfway through your life if you're betting on making it to 100. So get off your tush and go after what you want, what gives you joy, what fills your cup. Now. With luck, you're gonna get old anyway. The in-between part – the quality of your life moving forward – is up to you.

If you don't **seize the opportunity**, a decade or two from now you may be humming another Billy Joel song about it possibly being too late, "Turn the Lights Back On" – a great, but not necessarily happy, tune. I can't quote those lyrics, either. Rest assured that they are awesome. You can find them all over the internet.

Hope you laughed your way through my book and had one or two **AHA moments**. If you enjoyed it, stay on the lookout for my next book, subject still a state secret, but think the universe of social commentary. (Narrows it down, right?!)

In the meantime, please share this book with a friend (or better yet, buy them a copy) and check out my last book, "If You Give A Man A Tesla: A Parody."

Oh and finally – **if you liked this book, please leave a positive review on Amazon**. Those reviews really help us authors.

Thank you, dear reader. You are the best.

THE END

Made in United States
Troutdale, OR
11/14/2024

24820927R00031